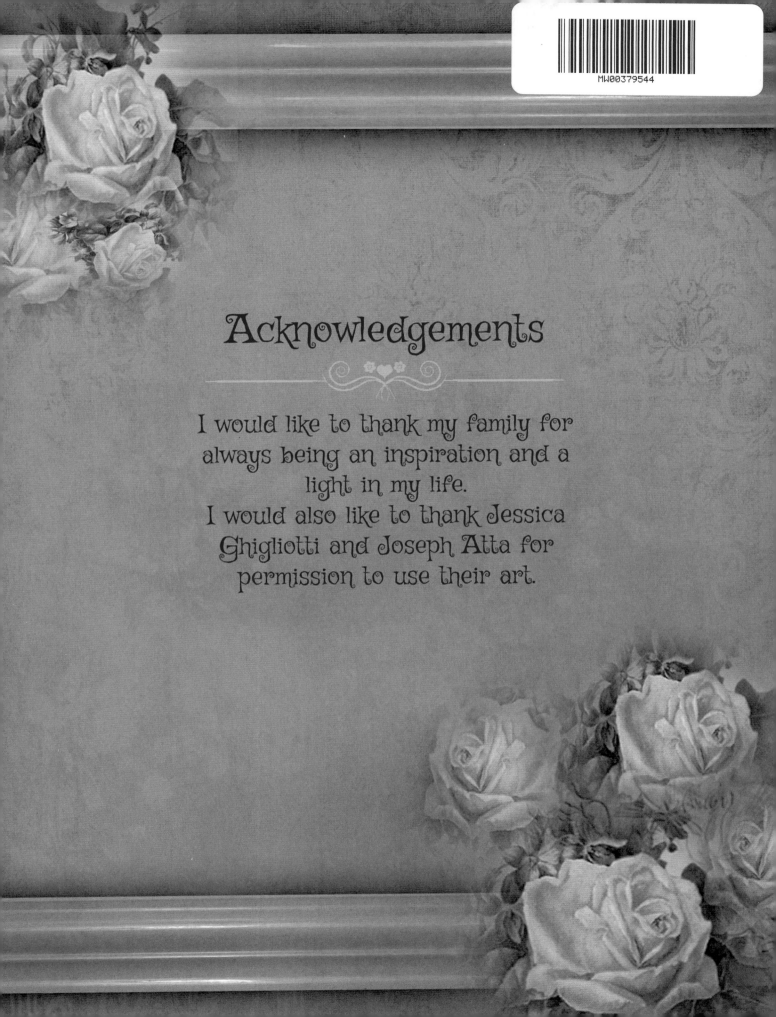

Acknowledgements

I would like to thank my family for always being an inspiration and a light in my life.
I would also like to thank Jessica Ghigliotti and Joseph Atta for permission to use their art.

EDITOR'S NOTE

Dear Catholic Girls,

I wish to inspire you, Catholic Maidens, to a greater life of virtue. In order to lead a life of virtue and piety, you need to work on having good, daily habits…habits that will become second nature to you.

Let me tell you a little secret to success in forming these daily habits in your life… It is in keeping a journal, a To-Do List! It will help you keep on track and stay focused each day.

This Catholic Girl's Traditional Journal is to encourage you on this journey! It will help you to accomplish goals on a daily basis. You will be checking off your spiritual activities, your chores and the other things you should try to accomplish each day as a good, Catholic girl. It also has places to write down things you are thankful for, the people you wish to pray for and other important parts of your day. These good habits will carry you through your life.

My hope for you is that, after you are finished this journal, you can pick up any empty journal and be able to write **YOUR OWN** To-Do List…and that this will become a pattern for the rest of your life. How much help you will gain in your vocation if you learn to do this!

Start now! Form those good habits! Draw from this journal an outline of what can be your To-Do List for the rest of your life!

For the next 30 days
(and hopefully for years to come)….
Happy Journaling!

Your 30-Day Daily Journal

Day 1

Thought for Today:
The most precious earthly treasure a girl can have is character. Her character is what she really is. If she will look beyond what she appears to be, and what people think of her, and look at her heart fairly and honestly, judging herself by the standards of right and wrong to which her own conscience gives sanction, then she can know whether she has a good character.
-Beautiful Girlhood, Mabel Hale, 1920's

I will offer my prayers, works, joys and sufferings today for:

_____

Spiritual Checklist
(Prayers from the Heart)

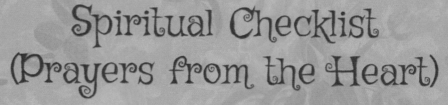

♡ Morning Prayers
♡ Spiritual Reading
♡ Rosary
♡ Night Prayers
♡ _____
♡ _____

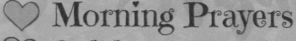

Everyday Checklist
* Chores
* 1 Kind Deed for a Family Member
* Homework/School/ Practice Instrument
* Smiled More

My Own To-Do List:
* _____
* _____
* _____

Check if you did a Spiritual/Corporal Work of Mercy
(Handed out a miraculous medal, visited the sick, said an extra prayer for someone, did a spiritual bouquet, etc.)

I'm Thankful For:

1 _____

2 _____

3 _____

Day 2

Thought for Today:

The girl who comes to perfect womanhood must learn to be obedient. Her whole life must be governed, not by whim or pleasure, but by right and duty. Her first lessons of obedience are learned at home. She becomes aware that all things are not for her personal convenience and pleasure, but that she must do her part in service, restraint, and sacrifice, that home may be orderly and happy.

-Beautiful Girlhood, Mabel Hale

I will offer my prayers, works, joys and sufferings today for:

Spiritual Book
that I am Reading Today:

_____

Spiritual Checklist
(Prayers from the Heart)

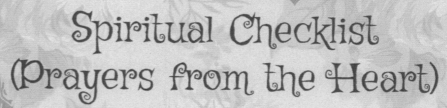

♡ Morning Prayers
♡ Spiritual Reading
♡ Rosary
♡ Night Prayers
♡ _____
♡ _____

This person made me happy today:

_____

Jesus, please bless him/her!

Everyday Checklist
❋ Chores
❋ 1 Kind Deed for a Family Member
❋ Homework/School/ Practice Instrument
❋ Smiled More

My Own To-Do List:
❋ _____
❋ _____
❋ _____

Draw My Day:

Day 3

Thought for Today:

You are known by your words. Speak kindly at all times. Do not listen to gossip. Let only good things come from your lips.

Ask Our Lady to help you with this. God will bless you if you try hard not to speak unkindly about others.

I will offer my prayers, works, joys and sufferings today for:

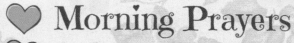

Spiritual Checklist (Prayers from the Heart)

♡ Morning Prayers
♡ Spiritual Reading
♡ Rosary
♡ Night Prayers
♡ _____
♡ _____

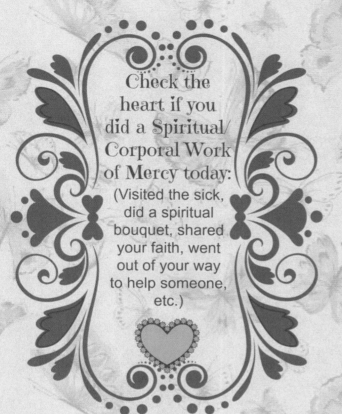

Check the heart if you did a Spiritual/Corporal Work of Mercy today: (Visited the sick, did a spiritual bouquet, shared your faith, went out of your way to help someone, etc.)

Everyday Checklist

* Chores
* 1 Kind Deed for a Family Member
* Homework/School/ Practice Instrument
* Smiled More

My Own To-Do List:

* _____
* _____
* _____

I'm Thankful For:

1 _____

2 _____

3 _____

Day 4

Thought for Today:

The shortsighted world is quite at fault when it pronounces the life of a nun joyless and more or less unhappy. She must, it is true, renounce much which men regard as pleasure and enjoyment, but only to be richly compensated for all she gives up by higher and purer joys.

All the sacrifices she may have to make do but increase her happiness; they cause her to partake more abundantly of that paeace of which Our Lord says: "My peace I give unto you; not as the world giveth do I give unto you."

Father Lasance, Catholic Girl's Guide

I will offer my prayers, works, joys and sufferings today for:

Spiritual Book that I am Reading Today:

_____

Spiritual Checklist (Prayers from the Heart)

♡ Morning Prayers
♡ Spiritual Reading
♡ Rosary
♡ Night Prayers

♡ _____

♡ _____

This person made me
happy today:

_____

Jesus, please bless
him/her!

Everyday Checklist
* Chores
* 1 Kind Deed for a
  Family Member
* Homework/School/
  Practice Instrument
* Smiled More

My Own To-Do List:
* _____
* _____
* _____

Draw My Day:

Day 5

Thought for Today:

Girls very much become like their friends. Choose your friends wisely. Good companions, ones that will help you get to heaven, are a treasure. Our Lord will help you find a good friend if you ask Him.

I will offer my prayers, works, joys and sufferings today for:

Be a good friend!

Spiritual Checklist (Prayers from the Heart)

♡ Morning Prayers
♡ Spiritual Reading
♡ Rosary
♡ Night Prayers
♡ _____
♡ _____

Check the heart if you did a Spiritual/ Corporal Work of Mercy today: (Visited the sick, did a spiritual bouquet, shared your faith, went out of your way to help someone, etc.)

Everyday Checklist
- ✳ Chores
- ✳ 1 Kind Deed for a Family Member
- ✳ Homework/School/ Practice Instrument
- Smiled More

My Own To-Do List:
_____
- ✳ _____

I'm Thankful For:

1 _____

2 _____

3 _____

Day 6

Thought for Today:

The virtue that counts for most in your life is purity of heart. How do you get and hold on to that virtue?

It is possible if you are careful what you put into your minds. The books you read, the movies you watch and the music you listen to will have a great impact on this virtue.

This purity of heart will be with us if we think good and pure thoughts. Sometimes this is hard, but we don't want to make it any harder than it is. Make sure and fill your mind with good and noble ideas. This will help you to be pure of heart.

"Blessed are the Pure of Heart, for they shall see God." (Matthew 5:8)

I will offer my prayers, works, joys and suffering today for:

♥♥♥♥♥♥♥♥♥♥♥♥♥♥♥♥♥♥♥♥♥♥

Spiritual Book that I am Reading Today:

_____

Good thoughts...

Spiritual Checklist (Prayers from the Heart)

♥ Morning Prayers
♥ Spiritual Reading
♥ Rosary
♥ Night Prayers
♥ _____
♥ _____

This person made me happy today:

_____

Jesus, please bless him/her!

Everyday Checklist
* Chores
* 1 Kind Deed for a Family Member
* Homework/School/ Practice Instrument
* Smiled More

My Own To-Do List:
* _____
* _____
* _____

Draw My Day:

Day 7

Thought for Today:
Your faith is the most precious thing you have. You must take care of it and help it to grow or you may lose it and lose heaven. Read about your faith, listen to sermons, listen to the wisdom of others and pray. This will help you grow in your faith.

I will offer my prayers, works, joys and sufferings today for:

_____

Spiritual Checklist
(Prayers from the Heart)

♡ Morning Prayers
♡ Spiritual Reading
♡ Rosary
♡ Night Prayers
♡ _____
♡ _____

Check the heart if you did a Spiritual/Corporal Work of Mercy today: (Visited the sick, did a spiritual bouquet, shared your faith, went out of your way to help someone, etc.)

Everyday Checklist
* Chores
* 1 Kind Deed for a Family Member
* Homework/School/Practice Instrument
* Smiled More

My Own To-Do List:
* _____
* _____
* _____

I'm Thankful For:

1 _____

2 _____

3 _____

Day 8

Thought for Today:

Learn to love nature. Look at the trees, the flowers, the birds, etc. They all show the magnificence of a loving God, who created all of them.
Take time in the outdoors to think about these things....and realize that God loves you more than all of these wonderful and beautiful things!

I will offer my prayers, works, joys and sufferings today for:

Spiritual Book
that I am Reading Today:

_____

Spiritual Checklist
(Prayers from the Heart)

♡ **Morning Prayers**
♡ **Spiritual Reading**
♡ **Rosary**
♡ **Night Prayers**
♡ _____
♡ _____

This person made me happy today:

_____

Jesus, please bless him/her!

Everyday Checklist
- Chores
- 1 Kind Deed for a Family Member
- Homework/School/ Practice Instrument
- Smiled More

My Own To-Do List:
- _____
- _____
- _____

Draw My Day:

Day 9

Thought for Today:

Do not be of the world. Be like Mary. Do your daily duties, obey, be happy, and have good fun. But don't forget, Mary took time to pray and be with God. She was so happy because God was Number One in her life. Do the same and you will have joy!

I will offer my prayers, works, joys and sufferings today for:

_____

_____

Spiritual Checklist (Prayers from the Heart)

♡ Morning Prayers
♡ Spiritual Reading
♡ Rosary
♡ Night Prayers
♡ _____
♡ _____

Check the heart if you did a Spiritual/ Corporal Work of Mercy today: (Visited the sick, did a spiritual bouquet, shared your faith, went out of your way to help someone, etc.)

Everyday Checklist
* Chores
* 1 Kind Deed for a Family Member
* Homework/School/ Practice Instrument
* Smiled More

My Own To-Do List:
* _____
* _____
* _____

I'm Thankful For:
1. _____
2. _____
3. _____

Thought for Today:

God is watching you at all times...not as someone who is stern, but as a loving and caring father.
He wants to see you grow into a happy and faith-filled Catholic adult one day.
He is happy to see you having good and wholesome fun.
It is important to Him that you talk to Him...about everything.
He is pleased when you go to His Mother, also.
Being a faithful Catholic makes the world a lot brighter place to be!

Day 10

I will offer my prayers, works, joys and sufferings today for:

Spiritual Book that I am Reading Today:
_____

Spiritual Checklist
(Prayers from the Heart)

♡ Morning Prayers
♡ Spiritual Reading
♡ Rosary
♡ Night Prayers
♡ _____
♡ _____

This person made me happy today:

_____

Jesus, please bless him/her!

Everyday Checklist
※ Chores
※ 1 Kind Deed for a Family Member
※ Homework/School/ Practice Instrument
※ Smiled More

My Own To-Do List:
※ _____
※ _____
※ _____

Draw My Day:

Day 11

Thought for Today:

Love your father and mother, love them from the depth of your heart, with true, filial affection. Always take delight in the society of your parents, and thus give external proof of the the love you bear them.
-Fr. Lasance

I will offer my prayers, works, joys and sufferings today for:

_____

Spiritual Checklist
(Prayers from the Heart)

♥ Morning Prayers
♥ Spiritual Reading
♥ Rosary
♥ Night Prayers
♥ _____
♥ _____

Check if you did a Spiritual/Corporal
Work of Mercy
(Handed out a miraculous medal, visited the sick,
said an extra prayer for someone, did a spiritual
bouquet, etc.)

Everyday Checklist
* Chores
* 1 Kind Deed for a
  Family Member
* Homework/School/
  Practice Instrument
* Smiled More

My Own To-Do List:
* _____
* _____
* _____

I'm Thankful For:

1 _____

2 _____

3 _____

Day 12

Thought for Today:
Christianity teaches us to regard work as something sacred, honorable, and exalted. Work is your duty.
You must not only value work very highly, you must also love it.
We are taught by daily experience that industrious, active girls who are fond of work are almost without exception virtuous and pure. Hence it follows that the highest praise which can be bestowed upon a girl is to say of her that she is industrious, never tired of work, but always usefully occupied.
–Fr. Lovasik, Catholic Girl's Guide

I will offer my prayers, works, joys and sufferings today for:

Spiritual Book
that I am Reading Today:
_____

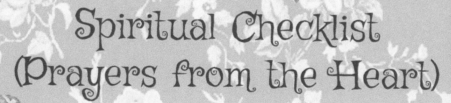

Spiritual Checklist
(Prayers from the Heart)

♡ Morning Prayers
♡ Spiritual Reading
♡ Rosary
♡ Night Prayers
♡ _____
♡ _____

This Person made me happy today:

_____

JESUS, PLEASE BLESS him/her!

Everyday Checklist
* Chores
* 1 Kind Deed for a Family Member
* Homework/School/ Practice Instrument
* Smiled More

My Own To-Do List:
* _____
* _____
* _____

Draw My Day:

Day 13

Thought for Today:

Work hard at making your home life pleasant. The family is a big part of the foundation of your happiness. Be nice to your brothers and sisters, do your chores well. You will be an example to others in your family and they will try harder. This will help to have a peaceful and joyous family life!

I will offer my prayers, works, joys and sufferings today for:

Spiritual Checklist (Prayers from the Heart)

♡ **Morning Prayers**
♡ **Spiritual Reading**
♡ **Rosary**
♡ **Night Prayers**
♡ _____
♡ _____

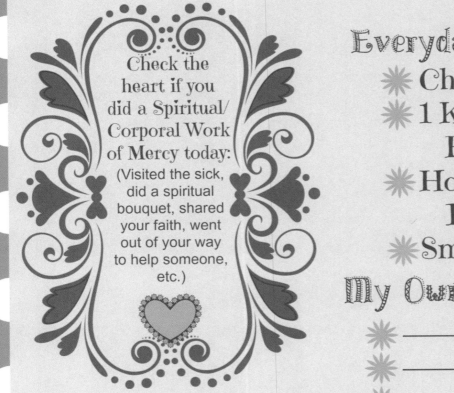

Check the heart if you did a Spiritual/Corporal Work of Mercy today:
(Visited the sick, did a spiritual bouquet, shared your faith, went out of your way to help someone, etc.)

Everyday Checklist
✳ Chores
✳ 1 Kind Deed for a Family Member
✳ Homework/School/Practice Instrument
✳ Smiled More

My Own To-Do List:
✳ _____
✳ _____
✳ _____

I'm Thankful For:
⭐1 _____
⭐2 _____
⭐3 _____

Day 14

Thought for Today:

Thank God for all the little things He gives us...our family, the weather, our school and everything else. He has given us life and we need to thank Him for that.
God is holding the world up and how much more will He hold us up each day!
Let us thank Him by saying our prayers better, by being kinder to everyone we meet, and by doing our chores well.
What a great way to thank God for all He does for us!

I will offer my prayers, works, joys and sufferings today for:

Spiritual Book that I am Reading Today:

_____

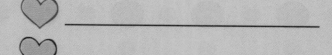

Spiritual Checklist (Prayers from the Heart)

♡ Morning Prayers
♡ Spiritual Reading
♡ Rosary
♡ Night Prayers
♡ _____
♡ _____

This person made me happy today:

_____

JESUS, PLEASE BLESS him/her!

Everyday Checklist
Chores
1 Kind Deed for a
Family Member
Homework/School/
Practice Instrument
Smiled More

My Own To-Do List:
_____
_____
_____

Draw My Day:

Thought for Today:

Read. Read lots. Make books your friends. Only pick books that are wholesome and good, for you will become like the books you read. Get your spiritual reading in each day. This will help you grow into a confident, Catholic young lady.

Day 15

I will offer my prayers, works, joys and sufferings today for:

Spiritual Checklist (Prayers from the Heart)

♡ Morning Prayers
♡ Spiritual Reading
♡ Rosary
♡ Night Prayers
♡ _____
♡ _____

Check the heart if you did a Spiritual/ Corporal Work of Mercy today: (Visited the sick, did a spiritual bouquet, shared your faith, went out of your way to help someone, etc.)

Everyday Checklist

- ✴ Chores
- ✴ 1 Kind Deed for a Family Member
- ✴ Homework/School/ Practice Instrument
- ✴ Smiled More

My Own To-Do List:

- ✴ _____
- ✴ _____
- ✴ _____

I'm Thankful For:

1 _____

2 _____

3 _____

Day 16

Thought for Today:

Thank God for all of your blessings each day. When you realize the many sufferings that others go through...not having a roof over their heads, enough to eat or not even having a Mom and Dad to care for them...then it is easy to be grateful for your life!

A spirit of thankfulness is very pleasing to God. And it makes you happy, too. It brings a smile to your lips and a song in your heart.

So practice each day being thankful for the little things and for the big things!

I will offer my prayers, works, joys and suffering today for:

♥♥♥♥♥♥♥♥♥♥♥♥♥♥♥♥♥♥♥♥♥♥♥

Spiritual Book that I am Reading Today:

_____

Thank you, God!

Spiritual Checklist (Prayers from the Heart)

♡ Morning Prayers
♡ Spiritual Reading
♡ Rosary
♡ Night Prayers
♡ _____
♡ _____

This person made me happy today:

_____

Jesus, please bless him/her!

Everyday Checklist
* Chores
* 1 Kind Deed for a Family Member
* Homework/School/Practice Instrument
* Smiled More

My Own To-Do List:
* _____
* _____
* _____

Draw My Day:

Day 17

Thought for Today:

Every girl owes it to herself and to her associates to be sunny. A happy girlhood is so beautiful that it cannot afford to be spoiled by needless frowns and pouts. There are clouds enough in life without making them out of temper.

A girl who is full of smiles and sunshine is a fountain of joy to all who know her. The world has enough of tears and sorrow at best, and her sweet, smiling face can scatter untold clouds. Could a girl ask for a better calling than that of a joy-maker for all about her?

-Beautiful Girlhood, Mabel Hale

I will offer my prayers, works, joys and sufferings today for:

_____

_____

Spiritual Checklist
(Prayers from the Heart)

♡ **Morning Prayers**
♡ **Spiritual Reading**
♡ **Rosary**
♡ **Night Prayers**
♡ _____
♡ _____

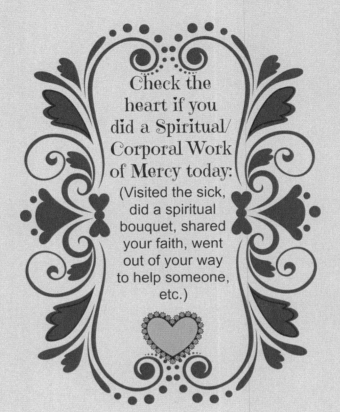

Check the heart if you did a Spiritual/ Corporal Work of Mercy today: (Visited the sick, did a spiritual bouquet, shared your faith, went out of your way to help someone, etc.)

Everyday Checklist

* Chores
* 1 Kind Deed for a Family Member
* Homework/School/ Practice Instrument
* Smiled More

My Own To-Do List:

* _____
* _____
* _____

I'm Thankful For:

1. _____
2. _____
3. _____

Day 18

Thought for Today:

One day, you will begin your vocation. You should not wait to prepare yourself for it...you must begin now.
Every girl should know how to cook.
You can learn to garden, to sew, to clean and all the other things that you will be doing no matter what vocation God asks of you.
Begin today! Strive towards being an accomplished young lady that is ready for her life's work!

I will offer my prayers, works, joys and sufferings today for:

Spiritual Book that I am Reading Today:

_____

Spiritual Checklist (Prayers from the Heart)

♡ Morning Prayers
♡ Spiritual Reading
♡ Rosary
♡ Night Prayers
♡ _____
♡ _____

This person made me happy today:

_____

Jesus, please bless him/her!

Everyday Checklist
* Chores
* 1 Kind Deed for a Family Member
* Homework/School/ Practice Instrument
* Smiled More

My Own To-Do List:
* _____
_____
_____

Draw My Day:

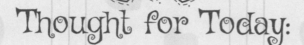

Day 19

Thought for Today:

Every day our girl will meet with circumstances in which she has her choice between frowning and sending back a stinging retort, or smiling and passing them by with a kind word. If she can pass these little bumps and keep sweet, then she has mastered the art of being sunny.
-Beautiful Girlhood, Mabel Hale

I will offer my prayers, works, joys and sufferings today for:

_____

_____

Spiritual Checklist (Prayers from the Heart)

♡ Morning Prayers
♡ Spiritual Reading
♡ Rosary
♡ Night Prayers
♡ _____

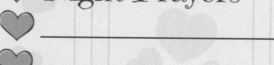

♡ _____

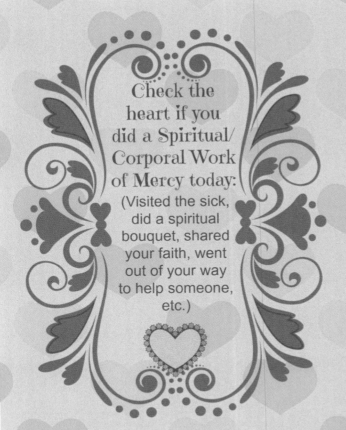

Check the heart if you did a Spiritual/Corporal Work of Mercy today:
(Visited the sick, did a spiritual bouquet, shared your faith, went out of your way to help someone, etc.)

Everyday Checklist
* Chores
* 1 Kind Deed for a Family Member
* Homework/School/ Practice Instrument
* Smiled More

My Own To-Do List:
* _____
* _____
* _____

I'm Thankful For:
1 _____
2 _____
3 _____

Day 20

Thought for Today:

The girl who is learning day by day to be a good daughter at home and a good sister to the young children, is also learning day by day how to make, in time, a good wife and a good mother. She is getting ready for one of the greatest works a woman can do. How beautiful for any woman is the work of making a good, true home for somebody! Every truly beautiful character is at its best at home. Let us never neglect the home life.

Beautiful Girlhood, Mabel Hale
(Paraphrased)

I will offer my prayers, works, joys and sufferings today for:

Spiritual Book
that I am Reading Today:

_____

Spiritual Checklist
(Prayers from the Heart)

♥ Morning Prayers
♥ Spiritual Reading
♥ Rosary
♥ Night Prayers
♥ _____
♥ _____

This person made me happy today:

_____

Jesus, please bless him/her!

Everyday Checklist
* Chores
* 1 Kind Deed for a Family Member
* Homework/School/ Practice Instrument
* Smiled More

My Own To-Do List:
* _____
* _____
* _____

Draw My Day:

Day 21

Thought for Today:

Be pure of heart. Guard your eyes from immodest images. Guard your ears from impure words. Keep your sweet innocence of mind and heart and you will be happy. Our Lady will smile upon you and God will bless you with a bright future in this life and in the next!
St. Joseph, Pure of Heart, pray for us!

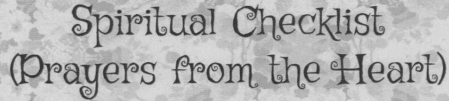

I will offer my prayers, works, joys and sufferings today for:

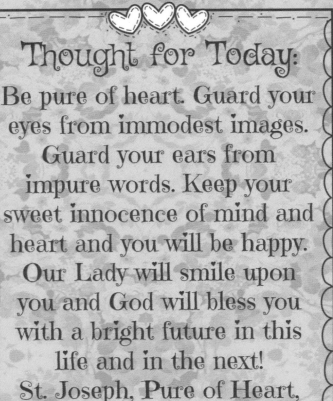

Spiritual Checklist
(Prayers from the Heart)

- ♡ Morning Prayers
- ♡ Spiritual Reading
- ♡ Rosary
- ♡ Night Prayers
- ♡ _____
- ♡ _____

Everyday Checklist

* Chores
* 1 Kind Deed for a Family Member
* Homework/School/ Practice Instrument
* Smiled More

My Own To-Do List:

* _____
* _____
* _____

Check if you did a Spiritual/Corporal Work of Mercy
(Handed out a miraculous medal, visited the sick, said an extra prayer for someone, did a spiritual bouquet, etc.)

I'm Thankful For:

1 _____
2 _____
3 _____

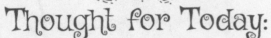

Day 22

Thought for Today:

When a girl is a Catholic, she knows where to go for strength and courage. She knows the Church is her stronghold and the Sacraments are the means to help her become holy. She often finds a quiet place where she can talk to God because she knows the power of prayer. Every girl has temptations...thoughts that will come that are not right. But she will turn to her mother, Mary, to help her to resist these evils and she will be given strength. She will therefore keep her life clean and pure. The more she trusts in God and His Blessed Mother, the more beautiful her life will be.

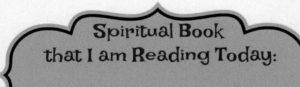

I will offer my prayers, works, joys and sufferings today for:

Spiritual Book that I am Reading Today:

_____

Spiritual Checklist (Prayers from the Heart)

- ♥ Morning Prayers
- ♥ Spiritual Reading
- ♥ Rosary
- ♥ Night Prayers
- ♥ _____
- ♥ _____

This person made me happy today:

_____

Jesus, please bless him/her!

Everyday Checklist
* Chores
* 1 Kind Deed for a Family Member
* Homework/School/ Practice Instrument
* Smiled More

My Own To-Do List:
* _____
* _____
* _____

Draw My Day:

Thought for Today:
Live in the sunshine.
Look on the bright
side, for there is
always a bright side.
No matter how a girl
is situated in life, she
can find something to
be thankful for.

-Beatiful Girlhood,
Mabel Hale

Day 23

I will offer my prayers, works, joys
and sufferings today for.

Spiritual Checklist
(Prayers from the Heart)

♡ Morning Prayers
♡ Spiritual Reading
♡ Rosary
♡ Night Prayers
♡ _____
♡ _____

Check the heart if you did a Spiritual/ Corporal Work of Mercy today: (Visited the sick, did a spiritual bouquet, shared your faith, went out of your way to help someone, etc.)

Everyday Checklist
* Chores
* 1 Kind Deed for a Family Member
* Homework/School/ Practice Instrument
* Smiled More

My Own To-Do List:
* _____
* _____
* _____

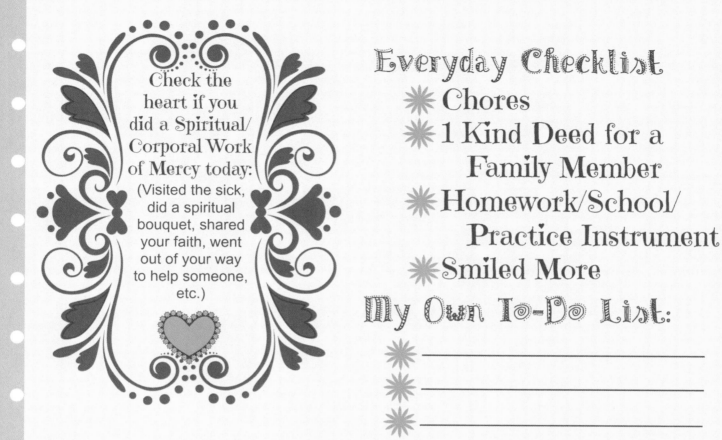

I'm Thankful For:

1 _____

2 _____

3 _____

Thought for Today:

Why are we so unhappy at times? Why do we find it so hard to be good and to get along with others? A lot of the times it is our venial sins that weigh us down. We need to get to Confession and clean our souls with Jesus' forgiving power. We get so much more help from Our Lord when we go to Confession often. Then, it becomes easier to be good...and to be joyful!

Day 24

I will offer my prayers, works, joys and sufferings today for:

♥♥♥♥♥♥♥♥♥♥♥♥♥♥♥♥♥♥♥♥♥♥♥

Spiritual Book that I am Reading Today:

_____

Spiritual Checklist (Prayers from the Heart)

♡ Morning Prayers
♡ Spiritual Reading
♡ Rosary
♡ Night Prayers
♡ _____
♡ _____

This person made me happy today:

_____

Jesus, please bless him/her!

Everyday Checklist
* Chores
* 1 Kind Deed for a Family Member
* Homework/School/Practice Instrument
* Smiled More

My Own To-Do List:
* _____
* _____
* _____

Draw My Day:

Day 25

Thought for Today:

God knows everything. So, don't ever feel that God is far away! God is very close to you. God is near you always. Oh, I know that some days things go wrong. But when things do go wrong, don't get the idea that God has gone back on you!

Remember, God is running this world, and He does things in the way that He knows to be the best way. So, just leave everything to Him! God has been running this world for thousands of years. He knows His business, and He never makes a mistake.
-Fr. Gerald T Brennan, 1950's

I will offer my prayers, works, joys and sufferings today for:

_____

_____

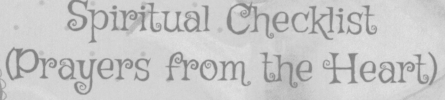

Spiritual Checklist
(Prayers from the Heart)

♡ Morning Prayers
♡ Spiritual Reading
♡ Rosary
♡ Night Prayers
♡ _____
♡ _____

Check the heart if you did a Spiritual/Corporal Work of Mercy today: (Visited the sick, did a spiritual bouquet, shared your faith, went out of your way to help someone, etc.)

Everyday Checklist
- ☀ Chores
- ☀ 1 Kind Deed for a Family Member
- ☀ Homework/School/ Practice Instrument
- ☀ Smiled More

My Own To-Do List:
- ☀ _____
- ☀ _____
- ☀ _____

I'm Thankful For:

1 _____

2 _____

3 _____

Thought for Today:

Your brothers and sisters should be your best friends. It is up to you to help that friendship grow.
We should not be nice to only those outside the home. It is important that we are pleasant to those we rub shoulders with each day.
We need to be unselfish, self-forgetful, thoughtful, kind, tender, patient and helpful.
We will win the hearts of our brothers and sisters this way. And brothers and sisters make the best of friends!

Day 26

I will offer my prayers, works, joys and sufferings today for:

♥♥♥♥♥♥♥♥♥♥♥♥♥♥♥♥♥♥♥♥♥♥

Spiritual Book
that I am Reading Today:

_____

Spiritual Checklist
(Prayers from the Heart)

♡ Morning Prayers
♡ Spiritual Reading
♡ Rosary
♡ Night Prayers
♡ _____
♡ _____

This person made me
Happy Today:

_____

Jesus, please bless
him/her!

Everyday Checklist
* Chores
* 1 Kind Deed for a
   Family Member
* Homework/School
* Practice Instrument
* Smiled More
My Own To-Do List:

* _____
* _____
* _____

Draw My Day

Day 27

Thought for Today:

You are a young lady and obedience is very important to learn now. When you become a young woman and choose a vocation, whether it be the religious life or a wife and mother, obedience is a very important virtue for both of these vocations. The more you learn to be obedient now, the easier it will be later in life and the sweeter your life will be. St. Francis de Sales says that he who is obedient will live sweetly and will be like a child in the arms of his mother, free from worry and from care. That's a pretty awesome promise!

I will offer my prayers, works, joys and sufferings today for:

_____

Spiritual Checklist (Prayers from the Heart)

♡ **Morning Prayers**
♡ **Spiritual Reading**
♡ **Rosary**
♡ **Night Prayers**
♡ _____
♡ _____

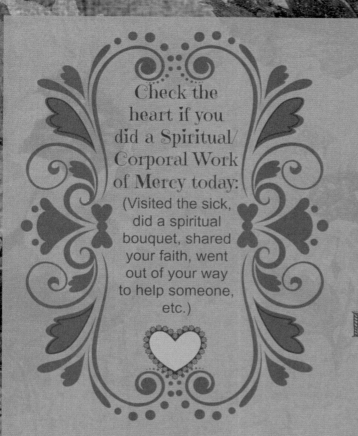

Check the heart if you did a Spiritual/ Corporal Work of Mercy today: (Visited the sick, did a spiritual bouquet, shared your faith, went out of your way to help someone, etc.)

Everyday Checklist
- ❊ Chores
- ❊ 1 Kind Deed for a Family Member
- ❊ Homework/School/ Practice Instrument
- ❊ Smiled More

My Own To-Do List:
- ❊ _____
- ❊ _____
- ❊ _____

I'm Thankful For:
1. _____
2. _____
3. _____

Thought for Today:

When we are good Catholics, we sometimes stand out from the rest of the crowd. We can feel like a fish out of water. But that's okay. We don't want to "follow the crowd" if they are going on a path that leads away from God.

Standing up for our faith takes courage but it is greatly rewarded by Our Lord. We feel peace in our hearts, we have a deep joy. We also grow in our faith and are a good example to others.

Most importantly, we will end our lives by joining Jesus and Mary in heavenly bliss!

Day 28

I will offer my prayers, works, joys and sufferings today for:

♥♥♥♥♥♥♥♥♥♥♥♥♥♥♥♥♥♥♥♥♥♥♥♥

Spiritual Book that I am Reading Today:

_____

Spiritual Checklist (Prayers from the Heart)

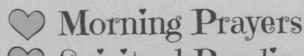

♡ **Morning Prayers**
♡ **Spiritual Reading**
♡ **Rosary**
♡ **Night Prayers**
♡ _____
♡ _____

This person made me happy today:

_____

Jesus, please bless him/her!

Everyday Checklist
Chores
1 Kind Deed for a Family Member
Homework/School/ Practice Instrument
Smiled More

My Own To-Do List:

_____

_____

_____

Draw My Day:

Thought for Today:

Always say your morning and night prayers. Don't put them off, they are too important. They are like the "Bookends" that hold up the rest of the day. We need God's blessing upon our day and upon our night. So make this a habit each day!

Day 29

I will offer my prayers, works, joys and sufferings today for:

_____

Spiritual Checklist (Prayers from the Heart)

♡ Morning Prayers
♡ Spiritual Reading
♡ Rosary
♡ Night Prayers
♡ _____
♡ _____

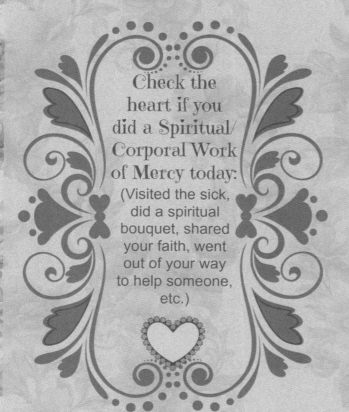

Check the heart if you did a Spiritual/ Corporal Work of Mercy today: (Visited the sick, did a spiritual bouquet, shared your faith, went out of your way to help someone, etc.)

Everyday Checklist
* Chores
* 1 Kind Deed for a Family Member
* Homework/School/ Practice Instrument
* Smiled More

My Own To-Do List:
* _____
* _____
* _____

I'm Thankful For:

1. _____
2. _____
3. _____

Thought for Today:

Make the saints your friends. They want to help, you just have to ask them. Especially pray to your patron saint...each day.
The saints are powerful with God and He wants to answer your prayers through them.

Day 30

I will offer my prayers, works, joys and sufferings today for:

Spiritual Book that I am Reading Today:

_____

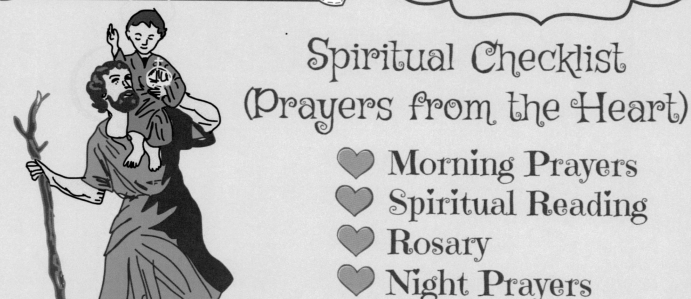

Spiritual Checklist (Prayers from the Heart)

- ♥ Morning Prayers
- ♥ Spiritual Reading
- ♥ Rosary
- ♥ Night Prayers
- ♥ _____
- ♥ _____

This person made me happy today:

_____

Jesus, please bless him/her!

Everyday Checklist

* Chores
* 1 Kind Deed for a Family Member
* Homework/School/Practice Instrument
* Smiled More

My Own To-Do List:

* _____
* _____
* _____

Draw My Day:

CONGRATULATIONS!

You have finished your 30-Day Journal and now you can start your own!

It doesn't have to be as fancy as this one....writing down the things you wish to accomplish each day is the important thing.

Make sure your spiritual acitivities are on the top of the list!

God bless you!

Well done!

Mrs. Leane VanderPutten lives in rural Kansas with her husband of thirty-three years. She is the mother of eleven children and has thirty grandchildren.
Her family is devoted to Tradition within the Fold of the Catholic Church, homsechoolers with five children still at home.
Their family life is lively, full of faith and joy!

For more copies of
The Catholic Girl's Traditional Journal go to
www.meadowsofgrace.com or amazon.com

Made in the USA
Monee, IL
16 December 2020